W9-AQK-826

Put Beginning Readers on the Right Track with
ALL ABOARD READING™

The All Aboard Reading series is especially for beginning readers. Written by noted authors and illustrated in full color, these are books that children really and truly *want* to read—books to excite their imagination, tickle their funny bone, expand their interests, and support their feelings. With four different reading levels, All Aboard Reading lets you choose which books are most appropriate for your children and their growing abilities.

Picture Readers—for Ages 3 to 6
Picture Readers have super-simple texts, with many nouns appearing as rebus pictures. At the end of each book are 24 flash cards—on one side is the rebus picture; on the other side is the written-out word.

Level 1—for Preschool through First-Grade Children
Level 1 books have very few lines per page, very large type, easy words, lots of repetition, and pictures with visual "cues" to help children figure out the words on the page.

Level 2—for First-Grade to Third-Grade Children
Level 2 books are printed in slightly smaller type than Level 1 books. The stories are more complex, but there is still lots of repetition in the text, and many pictures. The sentences are quite simple and are broken up into short lines to make reading easier.

Level 3—for Second-Grade through Third-Grade Children
Level 3 books have considerably longer texts, harder words, and more complicated sentences.

All Aboard for happy reading!

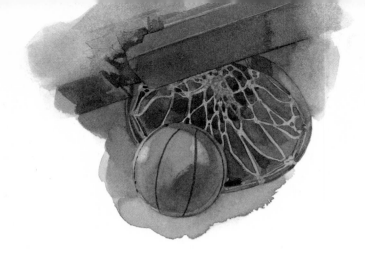

Thanks to the Naismith Memorial Basketball Hall of Fame.

Photo credits: back cover, Allsport; p.15, Doug Pensinger/Allsport; p.25, Jonathan Daniel/Allsport; p.37, Doug Pensinger/Allsport; p.48, Jed Jacobsohn/Allsport.

Library of Congress Cataloging-in-Publication Data

Kramer, Sydelle.
  Hoop heroes : Hardaway, Hill, Marbury, Ewing / by S.A. Kramer ; illustrated by Ken Call.
    p.   cm.—(All aboard reading. Level 3)
  Summary: Presents the lives, playing statistics, and basketball careers of Patrick Ewing, Penny Hardaway, Grant Hill, and Stephon Marbury.
  1. Basketball players—United States—Biography—Juvenile literature. 2. National Basketball Association. [1. Basketball players.] I. Call, Ken, ill. II. Series.
GV884.A1K728 1998
796.323'092'273—dc21   98-16769
[B]   CIP
                                                                                   AC
ISBN 0-448-41883-5 (GB) A B C D E F G H I J
ISBN 0-448-41647-6 (pb) A B C D E F G H I J

ALL
ABOARD
READING™

Level 3
Grades 2-3

HOOP HEROES

By S. A. Kramer
Illustrated by Ken Call

With photographs

Grosset & Dunlap • New York

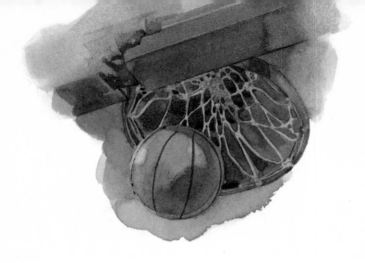

Mr. Magic

Anfernee "Penny" Hardaway is delighted. His rookie dream has just come true. It's June 30, 1993, and he's been traded to the Orlando Magic. But Penny's in for a shock. Down in Florida, there's trouble brewing.

Inside Orlando Arena, eight thousand people are booing. The Magic's general manager has just announced the trade.

The fans are angry. Most of them have never heard of Penny. The player he was traded for is popular. Nobody believes the general manager when he promises, "Your jeers will turn to cheers."

By the time the season begins, Penny's dream has turned into a nightmare. Whenever he takes the court, he gets booed. If he misses even one shot, the fans get on him. A shy, sensitive guy, he can't shrug it off.

Still, Penny's never been a quitter. All his life, he's had to overcome problems. When he was a baby in Memphis, Tennessee, his father left home and never came back. His mother was a singer who often performed out of town. So Penny went to live with his grandmother. He says, "It was hard at first, because I felt like no one really wanted me."

He and his grandmother grew close.
She was the one who nicknamed him
Penny. Since she didn't have much
money, they lived in a bad neighborhood.
She worried about Penny all the time. So
she made a rule that he could stay out
late only if he was in school or on the
court.

Penny started playing basketball as soon as he could hold a ball. It turned out he was a natural. By the time he was in high school, he was an All-American. In 1990, a magazine named him the high school player of the year. All through Memphis, fans treated him like a hero.

Because of his athletic skill, he had his pick of colleges. But Penny didn't want to be far from his grandmother. So he decided to go to nearby Memphis State.

When he first arrived at the school, Penny seemed to care only about basketball. He didn't bother to study. Soon he was failing tests. Finally his grades got so low, he wasn't allowed on the court for the rest of the season. In college, athletes can't compete in sports unless they keep up a certain average.

Penny was embarrassed. He said, "People looked at me like I was dumb." He made up his mind that he'd never get bad grades again. And he didn't. By his third year in college, Penny was an honor student. Of all the players on his team, he had the highest average.

Studying hard didn't change the way he played the game. At six foot seven he was tall for a guard, but as quick as a smaller man. He seemed to be everywhere on the floor and to see every single thing that happened. If he wasn't shooting a three-pointer or grabbing a rebound with his high jump, Penny was throwing a great bounce pass or dunking off the alley-oop.

But his troubles weren't over. Something terrible happened to him. Walking through his old neighborhood, he was robbed at gunpoint. The thieves jumped into a car, and fired off some shots. One bullet smashed off the sidewalk and into Penny's right foot.

The bullet broke three bones. Worse, it got stuck in a sensitive spot. If the doctor tried to take it out, Penny's foot could be damaged. He might never be able to play basketball again.

There was one chance. The doctor said the bullet just might shift to a place where it could be easily removed. Penny would have to wait and see.

A long six months went by. At last the bullet did shift and Penny had the operation. Amazingly, he was as good as new.

In 1993, Penny left college early for the NBA. It seemed that he was on his way to a great basketball career.

But now Magic fans are against him. It looks as if his bad luck is back. Somehow he's got to prove the trade is good for the team.

As the weeks pass, Penny plays his heart out in each game. Running the team on the floor, he gets the fast break going. A daring player, he often throws the no-look pass. Because he always knows where his teammates are, he hits the open man.

Slowly Orlando fans start appreciating Penny. After one game in November, the crowd gives him a standing ovation. Some people hold up a banner that says, "We Picked the Right One Baby, Uh-huh." By the end of the season, Penny is voted the Magic's most popular player.

His rookie success is just the beginning. With Penny on their side, the Magic makes the play-offs four straight years. A three-time All-Star, Penny becomes the team's scoring leader. One coach says, "He has simply proved to be one of the game's very best."

Nobody boos Penny now.

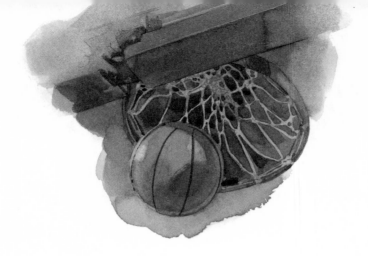

The Gentleman

Grant Hill grabs the inbounds pass. He has two seconds to tie the game or it will be all over. It's January 18, 1997, in Los Angeles, California. The Lakers lead Grant's Detroit Pistons, 80-77. Somehow Grant's got to score a three-pointer to push the game into overtime.

He doesn't waste an instant. With sweat dripping down his muscular arms, he dribbles fast into center court. From thirty feet out, he throws the ball at the basket. Just as the buzzer sounds, it drops through the net.

Tie! The seventeen thousand Laker fans fall silent. Once again, Grant has saved a game.

The Lakers never recover. Grant and the Pistons beat them in double overtime, 100-97. Grant finishes with a triple-double—34 points, 14 assists, and 15 rebounds. Some experts say it's the season's best individual performance.

At six foot eight, Grant is one of the NBA's best forwards. Detroit's leader, he's nicknamed "The Man."

But he is more than a terrific athlete. He's also a special person. He never plays dirty, talks trash, or shows off. If a ref makes a bad call, he doesn't get angry. Grant wants to win more than anything, but he wants to win fairly. He's the nicest guy in the game.

Even as a kid in Reston, Virginia, he was quiet and polite. His family had money, but he didn't want his schoolmates to find out. He said he "just wanted to blend in."

Grant was proud that his dad was a famous Dallas Cowboy star. But he was also embarrassed. In the eighth grade, he wouldn't come to a talk his dad gave in his school. Faking illness, he hid in the nurse's office. Grant explained, "I didn't want to seem better than everybody else."

An only child, Grant was close to his parents. But they didn't spoil him. His mom was so strict, his friends called her "The Sergeant." Grant wasn't allowed to get phone calls during the week. His TV watching was limited. Until he was sixteen, he couldn't go to parties.

His dad encouraged Grant to play sports. Soccer was Grant's favorite.

But by twelve he'd grown too tall for the game. His six-foot body was meant for basketball. He was the only ninth-grader to make his high school team.

Grant took basketball very seriously. He watched videotapes of superstars and imitated their moves. His goal was to be as good on the court as his dad was on the field.

He was. By the time he graduated, he'd scored over two thousand points. An All-American, he led his high school team to two state championships.

At Duke University, Grant was an even bigger star. Once again he was an All-American, making Duke's team his very first year. Named 1992's best defensive college player, Grant led Duke to back-to-back National Collegiate Athletic Association (NCAA) titles.

After graduation, he joined the
Pistons. In his very first game, he scored
25 points and had 10 rebounds and 5
assists. It was a sign of things to come.

No one could go from the dribble to
the dunk faster. He was as graceful as a
dancer when he glided to the basket.
With his long stride and quick, high
jump, he could dart through any defense.

As a twenty-two-year-old rookie, Grant became the NBA's most popular player. Known as "Mr. Nice Guy," he got so much fan mail, he had to hire someone to answer it. Wherever he played, crowds cheered him on.

But Grant found out it was hard being popular. Since fans always mobbed him outside, he stayed home most of the time. To have fun, he filled a big room with video arcade games. He even cut his own hair so he wouldn't have to go out.

In the 1994-95 All-Star Game, Grant was the top vote getter. It was the first time a rookie had ever finished first. Ever modest, he said, "It doesn't seem right."

That was just the first of many NBA honors. In 1995, Grant shared the Rookie of the Year award with Jason Kidd. After only three years in the NBA, he was ninth on the all-time triple-doubles list.

Today Grant's one of the most famous athletes in the world. But he won't be satisfied until he's number one. He says, "I mean business. I think I can be the best player in the NBA." Piston fans are sure he's right.

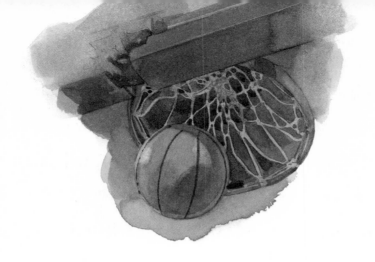

Starbury

Minneapolis, Minnesota. December 26, 1996. It's a big night for rookie point guard Stephon Marbury. His Minnesota Timberwolves are in action against the New York Knicks. When Stephon was a kid, the Knicks were his favorite team. Now he's on the court against them for the very first time.

But some experts feel Stephon should not be playing pro ball. He's too young, they say—only nineteen years old. They think he doesn't have enough experience—he's played just a single year of college ball. How can he be ready for the NBA?

But Stephon is sure the experts are wrong. Even as a child, he believed in himself. He started playing the game with his older brothers when he was just three. Although they were talented athletes, they never made it to the NBA. To help Stephon do what they couldn't, they taught him well.

Of course, Stephon had great talent,
too. By the age of six, he could shoot and
dribble with both hands. At nine, he put on
halftime shows during high school games.

As he threw up three-pointers, he'd yell "Bye-bye, birdie." His shots were so accurate, the net barely moved.

Soon people were talking about Stephon all over his hometown, Brooklyn, New York. His brothers were thrilled. So were his parents. They believed basketball was the key to his future—and a better life for them all.

The Marburys hated the run-down housing project where they lived. A poor family, they couldn't afford a couch or extra chairs. When friends came to visit, they had to stand. Stephon's basketball skills might be their way out of poverty. Stephon knew his family was counting on him. So even though he was just a kid, he pushed himself hard.

Sometimes he shot hoops in the playground until two in the morning. To stay in shape, he'd race up and down fifteen flights of stairs, three times in a row.

By the time he was eleven, Stephon was a local star. When he scored 41 points in one game, New York newspapers reported it. Experts called him America's best sixth-grade basketball player. College teams trained their eyes on him. In high school, Stephon was a starting player in his first year. He was only five foot nine, but he handled the ball better than anyone. The complete point guard, he could pass, steal, shoot, and run the team. Unselfish, he knew his job was to get the ball to the open man.

A cool customer on the court, Stephon
could look one way and pass the other.
His dribble was tricky—he'd slowly bounce
the ball, then suddenly blast by defenders.

If a big man blocked his path, Stephon steamed around him by scooting under his arms. Always on the run, he was careful to keep his teammates in the action.

But then Stephon's success went to his head. He was so full of himself, some of his own teammates disliked him. Once he even ordered a classmate to carry his books. Later he said, "I wasn't a very nice kid. I thought I was it." Yet as he got older, he calmed down. "I learned to treat everybody with respect," he said.

By the age of seventeen, Stephon was rated the top high school basketball player in the country. An All-American, he led his team to both the 1995 New York State and Public Schools Athletic League titles. One coach said Stephon was "the greatest high school point guard" ever.

He went to Georgia Tech University for just one year. After that, he joined the NBA to make money to help his family. Timberwolves fans welcomed him. They liked his style.

Even on the court, Stephon wore a diamond earring in each ear. Now six foot two, he decorated his arms with large tattoos. His baggy shorts looked big enough for the whole team to fit inside.

But tonight, Stephon's style hasn't impressed the Knicks. Right now, they're crushing the Timberwolves, 64-48, in the third quarter.

Suddenly, Stephon comes alive. Bending at the waist, he dribbles low to the floor. Cutting through the defense, he changes direction in midair. In just seven minutes, he scores 13 points. The Timberwolves are back in the game. The seventeen thousand fans go wild.

Stephon's on fire. With his special crossover dribble, he slams past one Knick guard. On the free-throw line, he slips past the other. Then he drives in for a reverse lay-up—tie!

The Timberwolves go on to an upset victory, 88-80. As the buzzer sounds, Stephon hurls the ball over his shoulder. He's scored 27 points, with 7 assists. Plus he's finished without a single foul.

That year, the Timberwolves make the play-offs for the very first time. The next year they do it again. Fans know the reason—Stephon Marbury.

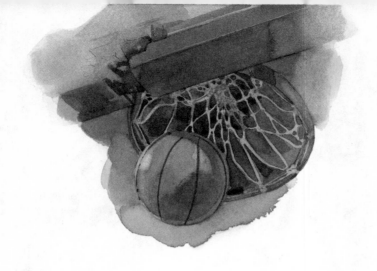

Big Guy

Cambridge, Massachusetts, 1975. Thirteen-year-old Patrick Ewing is puzzled. He's watching some boys play a very strange game. They keep trying to throw a big ball into a basket. Patrick's never seen anything like it before.

Patrick's been in America only a short while. He used to live on a Caribbean island called Jamaica. Soccer was the big sport there, but Patrick wasn't very good at it. He's beginning to wonder if he can play this new game.

Day after day, Patrick watches the boys shoot hoops in the playground. It looks easy enough. He knows his six-foot-one height will give him an edge. But nobody asks him to join in.

Then, one afternoon, the boys need an extra player. Suddenly, one of them spots Patrick and calls out, "Hey, do you want to play?" Patrick knows this is his chance. "Sure," he shouts.

He's terrible at the new game. He can't shoot or dribble. He feels clumsy on the court. Later he says, "It was more difficult than I could have imagined." But basketball is fun anyway. He makes up his mind he's going to master it.

Patrick practices hard. He learns how
to move with the ball, play defense, and
score. But a year later, he still can't dunk,
even though he's grown to six foot six.

Patrick doesn't give up. Slowly he gets better—and better. At fifteen, he's a tough defender who muscles his way to the basket. By sixteen, he's judged one of America's best high school players. Soon his fierce scowl and seven-foot body also make him one of the most feared.

Being so tall helps Patrick on the court. But off it, his height can be a problem. People stare at him. In school mean kids call him a freak.

That's not his worst problem at school. He's falling behind. He has trouble reading. To keep from failing, he studies with a tutor.

Other teams find out, and their fans call Patrick dumb. At games, they hold up signs saying, "Ewing Can't Read." Hollering that he's a monkey, they throw bananas on the court.

The insults make Patrick play harder. As he speeds down the floor, he sometimes points at the scoreboard. Fans know why he does that—his team is almost always ahead. With Patrick at center, his high school has a 74-1 record and wins three state titles.

But Patrick's basketball success doesn't make fans shut up. When he first plays for Georgetown University in 1981, the crowds flash posters saying "Ewing Is an Ape." Although he's now a good student, fans wear "Ewing Kan't Read Dis" T-shirts and buttons.

Opponents taunt Patrick, too, as they fight him for the ball. At first, he loses his temper. He even throws an occasional punch. But soon Patrick realizes he has to ignore the abuse. He's worked too hard at the game to let cruel insults get in his way. Playing tight defense, he becomes the toughest guy on the floor. His coach says, "Patrick is a warrior."

At Georgetown, Patrick is a basketball hero. Named All-American three times, he's the 1985 Player of the Year. His hometown holds a "Patrick Ewing Day" and gives him a key to the city. All the teasing and taunting are behind Patrick now.

He quickly becomes an NBA star for the New York Knicks. Named 1985-86 Rookie of the Year, he blocks shot after shot with his giant leaps. It's almost impossible to get by him when he's guarding the basket.

The Knicks build their team around
Patrick. It's a smart move—by 1989,
he's one of the NBA's top scorers. His
turnaround jumper nearly always goes in.
Teammates nickname him "Boomer"
because of his one-handed dunks.

Patrick is ferocious on the floor.
Opponents call him "the Beast of the
East." He's been known to slam the ball
in the basket and shout, "I'm a madman."

Off the court, he loves to laugh and
joke with teammates. But fans rarely see
that side of him. A private man, he hardly
talks to reporters and never signs
autographs.

He lets his achievements speak for
themselves. After all, Patrick's one of
only nineteen players to score over
21,000 career points. An All-Star
eleven times, he's been voted one of
the fifty greatest NBA players ever.
It's hard to believe there was a time
he hadn't even heard of the game.